Poetry to Fonder

Stephanie Harden

Table of Contents

These poems are made by my many Emotions.
Some of them are so far out I wonder my self
If I'm even here.

Some are from personal experiences from
my self and or my freinds.

This book is dedicated to my wonderful Childern
Thomas, Damian. You have been joys in my life.

Hope you all can understand or comprehend
the writings of this mind.

Sit back and Enjoy my Mind

Stephanie A Harden
June 16,2009

A loaded Gun

A
Cocked Loaded
Gun,
Instant tradedy found,
Reality locked in
time,
Sadness occurs again,
Innocence is lost
for you!

Rose

A rose thou it's thorns are painful,
Holds a beauty beneath its surface that
is fragile and tender,
Just like love,
It may hurt until you get past the thorns,
then its beautiful and wonderful

It's winter time again

It's wintertime again,
The frost fairies came last nite,
they danced across my windowpane,
With their ice skates,
leaving tiny figure eights
and prints from dew drop kisses,
laughing and giggling,
as they play
then went on their merry way,

It's wintertime again
see the cold wind blow
moving its arms across the open plains,
over the mountain peaks,
snatching the flowers and the leaves
and all the color from the trees,
Leaving skeletons in its wake
shivering in its cold winter arms

It's wintertime again,
one speck then two,
two specks then three,
watch the tiny snowflakes,
waltzing and swirling,
twirling and two stepping
watch them cover any color thats left,
one minute then two,
three minutes then four,
for any color left is no more
the earth is left white
looking pure and serene,

Its wintertime again,
standing by the window pane,
Snuggling in a blanket for two,
A fire in the hearth,
steaming cooca in hands
watching the changing...
as winter makes its stand nothing is said
just the soft melody of outdoors,
what a good place to be
inside and warm
why do you ask, answer is so clear cause
IT'S WINTERTIME AGAIN

Sacred Ground

Walking down a Marbled Path,
Beside a glimmering pool.
Sun so high
grass so green,
Looking peaceful and serene........
Birds a chirping, people talking.

Then up ahead to my right,
My eyes catch a half-fallen wall,
Then reality strikes me deep,
That on this ground I'm standing,
Stood a building 9 stories tall,
A bomb was planted,
Then went off.
Downed the building..
That once stood here on sacred ground.

Familes lost and Families cried,
on this ground I'm Standing on.
People come and People go.
Taking pictures just to show,
They stood on this sacred ground

I can feel.....
The pain, sorrow and the tears,
Echoing off the monument chairs,
for the souls lost,
on that day not so long ago.
My soul cries and my heart aches
Standing here on this sacred ground

Poetry to Ponder

Candle Light

Billion candle light,
banishes shadows,
fish surface then fades,
child fills a jar,
in spins.......
Tomorrow's Laughter

Upwards, Inwards, Outwards

Upwards, Inwards, Outwards.
changing lifetimes,
taking years,
reaching goals,
moon, stars
love, laughter,
found you out....
and with in

Touch of death

Dark sweeps over the room,
As a mist of musk fills his nostrils,
A feather touch of wonder
falls over his shoulder,
And a tingling feeling goes thru his body,
As fangs sink into his neck

Wheat

See the waves of wheat,
blowing in the field,
Watch the dark gray rain clouds,
Come blowing in,
As the rain comes Pounding,
Watch the wheat go down,
See the tear fall from his eyes,
As the farmer frowns

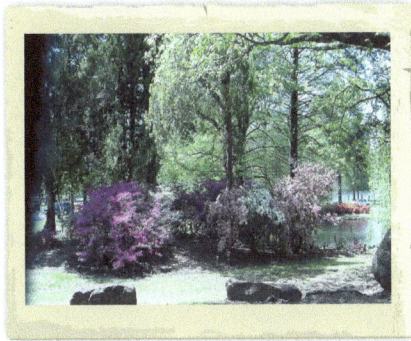

A Child's Whisper

We both stand here so fragile and small,
Watching and waiting,
Waiting and starring,
We wanted you to know,
Daddy we will always love you so,
We will never forget the tenderness...
That you gave,
As the flower fragance surrounds us..
We picture you standing with us,
As they lower you to rest,
We do our best to let the tears fall softly
No matter where we are at...
Your memory and your smile.
Will lead us through the lonely nights,
Will guide us through our toughiest fights,
Just cause we lay you to rest today,
Doesn't mean you went away,
You will always be here to stay,
In our hearts gently tucked away,
Cause we love you daddy,
For now and forever

Nakedguitar

Glide your fingers
over the long smooth neck
of this beauty,
slide your hand gently over her ribs,
slowly down over the shaply curved body,
feel the beat of past music,
pulse thru your fingers,
as you pick her up,
to see she fits perfectly in your hands,
against your body,
as you go to play her,
you see she is naked
the soul of her existance
is gone.......
she is stripped
of her strings, the once beautiful
guitar is no more.
so nakedguitar she is

Memories like

When I sit and think, that's when its starts
Memories, our special memories,

Memores like, When we threw our Little sister,
in the water hole in the front yard, OR..

Memories like, when we went fishing and I lost the
granddaddy, because I didn't tie the hook just right, OR..

Memories like, When we went wadding behind Uncle
bucks
cabin in the stream and we saw a gigantic slimy water
moccasin, brave you, tried to hook it with your stick
OR...

Mermories like, when we were fooling around and took
pictures of yourselfs, OR...

Memories like, when we dressed in green to graduate,
you in the 8th and me in the 12th,

But the best memory was when I got off the plane to
visit you 7 yrs ago. you at 9 yrs and me at 12. scared to
visit you for the first time,

But now we can't make any more memories, our special
memories, you, my brother and freind were taken away
from me.
you at 14 and me at 18.

I love you,
Stephanie
1986

Dedication Page in Loving memory of

"Memories Like"

This Poem was written in loving Memory
of
Jamy William Griffin.

Born: August 9th-1971

Gone to heaven with our lord

Feburary 22nd-1986

Gone but not forgotten.

God rest with you

Forever

Some say not to say forever,
Cause forever never ends,
But I say forever with you,
cause my heart is in it past the end,

Some say not to say forever,
Cause there is never a forever,
People change and go other ways,
but I say forever with you,
cause my soul is in it past the end

Some say not to say forever,
Cause forever is way to long
But I say forever with you,
Cause my love for you is that strong

Some say not to say forever,
Cause no one believes in forever
in this world today,
But I say forever with you
Cause in this world your more then forever
your everything I need,

Some say not to say forever,
but forever you are to me,
I love your forever
cause your more then eternity

Ocean Eyes

As blue as the ocean is,
The tender pool of your eyes are,
God of greece made them sparkle,
like the stars above,
As the sea god made them wild,
As the fierce hurricane winds,
But when i look.....
I see you,
the inner you, the tender you,
so peaceful, caring, so loving you,
That s what i see,
In the deep pool of your ocean eyes

Our Nation Shall Stand

Our Nation was stunned,
Our Nation did weep,
Our Nation was shocked by what it did see,
Many a people took a cause in their hands,
To destroy America for what it does stand,
Four mighty big birds,
of metal and steel
sweep down from the sky.....
bringing chaos and mayhem,
Destruction they did make,
The terrorist they did think,
That they brought America to its knees,
A tear did fall from the mighty eagle that day,
An ache in his soul and a hurt in his chest,
Our Nation was built on freedom,
There it stall stand,
Our nation was stunned ,
Our nation did weep,
But our Nation still stands proudly and strong..
for all to see,
This tragedy brought us together,
and not to our knees,
So all stand up and be proud,
That Americans are we,
Land of the mightly and land of the free,
For this united us and made us more strong...
Our Nation was stunned,
Our Nation did weep
But together we must stand and hold hands
and keep our land grand
and to keep it all free

Poetry to Ponder

Heart Endeavors

The heart endeavors,
the realm of a
enchanting bewitching land,
god's arrow soars to end
the wrath of rage

Ecstasy

Recalled memory of ecstasy,
tempting fragments of dreams,
Unrestrained tumbling snippets,
drifting remembrance,
scattered particles of surviving
unforgettable illusion

Wonder

Candles watch a
Glowing dark chilling sphere,
of orchestrated laughter,
shadows spins in and
banishes tomorrows light

Bassman

Is it fish or is it man,
you see it on the land,
see it in the water,
does it breath air, or
does it have gills,
what is it.. is it fish,
or man, all we know
it's called
THE BASSMAN

Adventurers are we

Grass, stumps
weed-grown lawns,
Juniper trees,
Indians, pirates,
Fences, walls, oceans,
crossing streets,
wept, laughed,
remember adventurers are
WE.

Foolishness

The laughter oozing,
menace, puzzled insightful
phrases,
he suddenly looks trapped above,
half soulless thoughts,
Delicious, posturing, portentous
talking

A Heart

Once there was a joyous heart,
full of rainbow color,
Then came one late summer night,
A wicked horrid thing,
It came and twisted...
A heart to pieces,
Cause of one mistake,
A weak moment in time,
And a joyous heart,
Lays in a throbbing ache,
Only two things and
time can tell..
If the twisted heart will heal,
If the joy will fil it
Full of rainbow color,
How I wish it were me...
to make it feel better

Game Nite

Game Nite...Coach

A pillar to some, a hero to many,
Watches as the team moves out,
A mother kisses her boy,
and wishes him luck
As another pats his rump and
one rustles his hair,
The star player,
From the side line,
WIth a clip board, held against his chest
the throw, the catch,
running, dodging,jumping
As he watches he moves to the players,
his eyes lite up... YARDS....FEET.
The light goes out as the player falls inches
from his goal.
THE TOUCHDOWN

Game Nite.... Mother

She kisses her boy, as he heads out,
Wishing him luck,
She watches as the ball is thrown,
He catches it,
Watching, wondering how he can move
like that,
this way that,
Holds her breath as a hunk of a man
Comes at him ,
As he jumps over a falling comrade that just
protected him,
She stands and screams as she watches
YARDS.....FEET.
OOH NO, Down just inches from his goal.
she aches in her heart
at his pain of not making it by inches

Game Nite .. continues

Game Nite....Player

Standing bundled like he is ready for war,
With knee pads, elbow pads, shoulder pads and
more,
He gets a pat on the rump and a rustle of his hair,
as his mama kisses him luck,
He runs with the rest to a field full of light,
Puts his helmet on and tightens his strap,
as the pigskin flies to his hands,
now he is ready to fight,
Dodging this way and there,
Jumping over a falling comrade,
Seeing the end so close but so far,
YARDS....FEET.
Then just inches he is down from his goal,
He sits there with his face in his hands,
As a team mate pats his back and says
"All will be right"

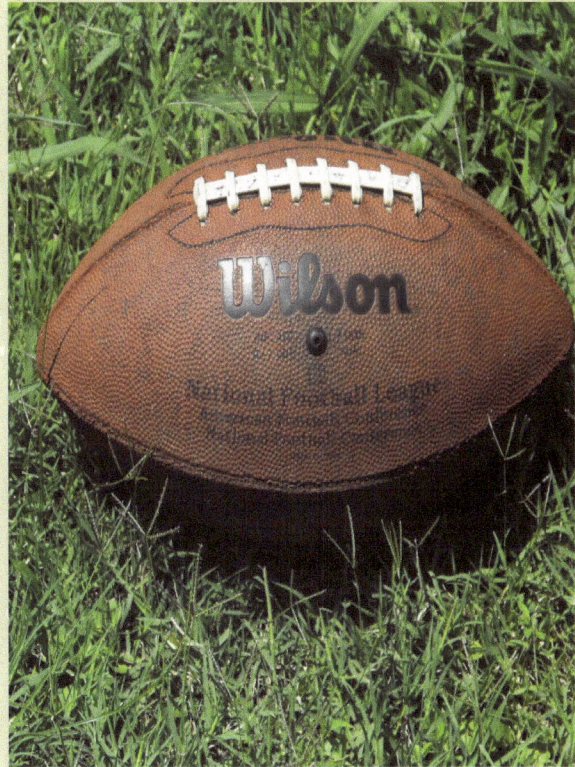

Longneck

Tall, slick , smooth,
sweat dripping from your body,
long slender neck,
Dressed in silver and red,
U make people happy,
U make people sad,
Ready to party at the drop of a hat,
You're the fun of the party,
No matter where you're at ,
Long Neck Bottle of Bud

Is it love?

Is it love, is it lust,
Is it the thought of two people together,
is it passion, is it nature,
is it the thought of two people together
is it touching, exploring,
is it the thought of two people together,
is .... it... love.... or.... lust.
two..words.. so.. close... but...so...Different.

Poetry to Ponder

Nightmare

Nightmare,
In the grip of nightmare,
U hear people scream,
toss and shake in the arms of nightmare,
but me, When I'm in the arms of nightmare,
It's a warm place to be
It's a secure place for me,
In the arms of nightmare,
Holds me tight, when I'm scared,
Makes me safe, the arms of nightmare

If I look in the eyes of freedom

If I look in the eyes of freedom,
can freedom.. pull me out of despair,
can freedom,,,, free me from my chains of fear,

If i look in the eyes of freedom,
will the feeling over power me,
the love , the caring, the sharing..
of his will,

If I look in the eyes of freedom,
will I see at last... IM FREE,,
flying, gliding, soaring,
on the wings of freedom

Rearview Mirror

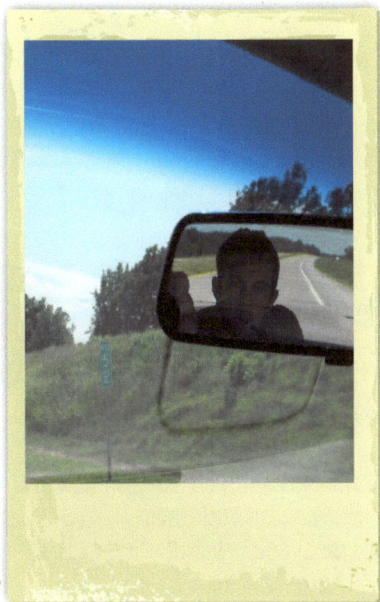

Driving down the wide open road
ALONE,
Not a worry on my mind,
Going 65 in a 55,
Suddenly I feel a hand,
Touch my shoulder,
Looks up into the rear-view Mirror,
There sits a young man,
As a chill goes thru me,
Words come to me from behind,
Like a plea,
"slow down Stephanie"
As by magic , my foot relaxes,
Drops from 65 to 55 in a flash,
As I look in the rear-view mirror,
he is gone,
As up ahead I hear a crash,
as metal hits metal
as I stop, Just the thought,
10 miles faster,
I'd be in the crash,
looks back in the rear-view,
he sits staring at me,
as a smile comes from him
and his hand touches my face,
He fades away in a state of
Grace

I'm not gone

Mama, It's me Mel,
As I see you crying for me,
I want to hold you tight,
Want to tell you "I love you"
and make it aahh so right,
Mama, As I see you're crying for me,
I want you to know
Mama I'm not gone
and you're not alone,
Mama, As I see you crying for me,
I want you to know,
I'm the dust dancing in the sunbeam,
I'm the springtime rain...
Falling on your skin,
I'm the warm summer breeze....
Blowing on your face,
I'm the multi-colored autumn leaf,
I'm the fresh crisp winter falling snow,
I'm in everything,
And everywhere you go,
So Mama please don't cry for me,
I'm not gone, and you're not alone

"Written for a co-workers Freind that lost her daughter
"Mel"
May you rest in peace
Wrote on June 16-2000

Fractured Mirror

Fractured mirror on the floor,
cracked like a spiders web,
As I look at myself,
In a lil Million pieces,
I wonder how many more
like me looked in it before,
What will it tell if it could?
Silhouettes of a lover's passion,
crying tears,
Many laughs,
How many died,
Reflections of so many souls,
Laying there,
Fractured mirror on the floor,
for the history is no more,
As you get swept up to throw out
with all the memories from
generations past pouring out,
fractured mirror to make no more.

Daddie's Pain

As a man sits staring out the window,
in the back yard is a child's swing,
swaying in the summer breeze,
a little truck on its side,

As a tear slides down his cheek,
wondering where the angels be,
As the trucks light comes straight on,
In a flash it's all gone,
His heart, soul and his Family

As the angel stands behind,
being there all that time,
A silence comes over the room,
the swing stops its sway,
As the teardrop is stilled,
By the sweet sound as the angel sings,

Ooh sweet child,
you might not believe,
I've been here all that time
taking in most of the
pain, hurt, sorrow ,
off your shoulders on to mine,

Ooh sweet child,
if only you knew,
how your family weeps for you,

ooh sweet child
You're not alone

Ooh sweet child
You're not alone

As a smaller hand reaches out,
The swing starts to sway about,
The teardrop sound is heard,
As he hears a soft echoing word,
"please daddy don't Cry, We're here by your
side"
A smile reaches his face,
as the sweet sound of the angel sings

Ooh sweet child
you might not believe
I've been here all the time,
Taking in most of the pain, hurt and sorrow
off your shoulders on to mine

ooh sweet child

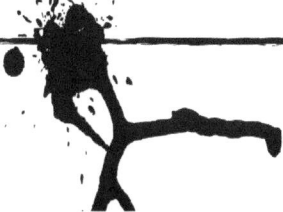

It seems like a million miles

It seems a million miles away,
My heart beats, my soul lives,
for the touch of his presence,
I open the door and blow a kiss...
on the cold winter north winds,
Watching it swirl and twirl as it goes...
over the trees,
under the bridges,
My kiss never gets smaller,
Just grows with passion,
looking for my love,
That is far away,
A door opens, and a man steps out,
Sensation hits him right on the lips,
A glow comes to his eyes,
And a smile to his mouth,
as he feels the kiss I sent,
He puts his hands to his lips,
Then presses them to his heart,
He can feel the heat from
so far way....
The touch of my lips as the kiss
touches out and reaches him...
He steps back in, closes the door,
thought of his love.....
so far away.

Like a dove

Like a dove,
cooing for its love,
so beautiful and peaceful,
Is my world when you're in it,
the cooing of its love song,
The beauty of its feathers,
Is like the love deep inside me,
the grace of its flight
gliding on the cool summer night,
Is how my love is for you,
like a dove
cooing for its love.

Mad

I'm so mad I see red,
I'm so mad my teeth are clinching tightly
I'm so mad this is the rest of my poem
juihot(*kljljlkjp;p?
jlkiop
ipk;lkjlkjoi)(u*(*-)(_{
)(_ol>ML
^tg..?
That is how mad I am right now,
Like to slam my fist into some persons
face.

Poetry to Ponder

Ice Wolf

Is it myth or is it real,
Is it a figment of your imagination?
Does it walk the earth, at night?
in your dreams, in your mind,
Can u feel of the wolfs icy fangs,
Hear the chill in his voice,
as it echoes off the ice,
Walking hunting for the souls
of the lonely.

5 senses

soft, cuddly, sweet, innocent...
Feel his struggle, feel his fear,
soft, cuddly, sweet, innocent...
Hear him whimper, her him weep,
soft, cuddly, sweet, innocent...
see him wiggle, see him giggle,
soft, cuddly, sweet, innocent...
Smell the newness, taste the joy,
soft, cuddly, sweet, innocent...
All is the birth of life,
soft, cuddly, sweet, innocent...

12/1999

"With a touch of a switch"

With a touch of a switch,
The Internet comes to LIFE.
World is at your finger tips.
You sit and stare
Looking at the names.
Wondering if they are doing the same.
Wondering if just a touch,
You can be zipped,
To another country,
To another place,
To another time.
Is it better ..... Is it worse?
Sitting here wondering.
Sitting here thinking.
With a touch of a switch,
The internet goes DEAD,
So does your connection to the world.

The warrior

Tiny daffodil

Time?

Silence

Poetry to Ponder

A poem can mean
one thing to some
and another thing
to others.

Life's Highway

Lifes highway, people think it's paved with gold,
but to be true its paved with ruts, bumps and
hurtles,

Lifes highway, has turns, curves and dead ends,
Life highway, lets you take one step forward
as it's winds push you two steps back,

Lifes highway, do you go on, do you stop?
If you could, would you start all over, change it,

LIfes highway, the hurtles are high, the hurtles
are low, that is lifes highway, do you jump,
do you crawl,

LIfes highway is never paved with gold,
if you are rich, if you are poor,
lifes highways always throws somthing in your
path, more for some, less for others,

Life highways do you jump or walk , live or die,
swim or drown or keep on moving, that is
lifes highway

Mirror of your soul

They say the eyes are the mirrors to your soul.
and when I look in yours...
There is so much to see,
Wonder, amusement, bewilderment and arousal,
Amusement: at my antics,
Bewilderment: seeing the crazy side, shy and ..
The wow I can't believe she did that or said that
side of me,
Arousal; on what I do to you when you're near me,
Your eyes tell me more then you want any one to
know,
And if you could see in mine,
You will see scared, shy, funny, arousal and
wonder and faithfulness,
Scared: of starting over,
Shy: as I'm shy
Funny: the little pixie in me wanting to play,
Wonder: how you feel about me.
Fatithfulness: is what I am to you faithful
true and true,
Baby look deep and see how I feel for you,
You will see it there in my green eyes,
Full of sparkles and life for you.

Thanksgiving

Once again the time hs come,
from near and far,
they did come,
Family, and freinds, comrades galore,
With hugs and kisses and laughter and
joy,

Once again the time has come,
to set the table
4 in all...
Plates and cups and silverware,

Once again the time has come.
the smell, the sight..
Golden brown the turkey is grand,
Heaps of potatoes, gravy and yams

In comes the stuffing in my papa's gentle hands,
out to the side the best part of all,
Smell...
the apple, cherry, mincement and pumpkin
all pies of course,

Once again the time has come,
We bow our heads,
Hands we do hold,
Praying for thanks and times we do share,
For this day has come and we all are here,
With the last amen,
we all dig right in,

Once again the time has come,
Family and freinds, comrades galore,

Happy Thanksgiving and many more.

Poetry to Ponder

Forbidden Love

Flying through my memory,
are past times of forbidden love,
two people belonging to another,
bodies longing to be together,
on that moonlight summer night,
baby , it felt so right,
to hold you aaahh so tight
on that moonlight summer night

By the sharing of all..

As i look in your eyes,
I see the lite of life and laughter,
It slowly seeps into my soul,
Pulling the sorrow and the pain out,
I can feel the heat of your smile..
Warm my blood as it melts the ice around my
heart
Opening it for your touch and tenderness,
New life starts to bloom around my heart,
Healing the wounds and the hurt,
As my soul feels the beauty of a two being one

The Photo

Through the eye of the lense,
sits the silhouette of an angel,
long blond hair,
flowing over naked breast,
that heat of the lamps,
fallin on naked thigh,
with a click of a switch,
a flash of a bulb,
the alter beauty is captured,
is it pornography... is it art,
It's in the eye of the taker,
take it or leave it,
it's beauty thru and thru

In a room full of people

In a room full of people,
sitting in my own lil world,
in a room full of people,
hear the noise,
here the silence,
in a room full of people,
how can one be alone,
in a room full of people,
feel the different powers,
feel the different vibes,
in a room full of people,
all alone
in a room full of people.

The Ride

Standing legs spread,
hovering over tons of raw energy,
nerves stretched,
adrenaline pumping,
hand raised,,, door opens,
Air crackles with excitement..
beast against man,
man against beast,
tossed, twisted,
right....left,
left....right,
5 seconds,
6,
7,
crowd screams
as the buller rider is tossed one last time,
to the victor... goes the beast.

Silence

Listen, what do you hear,
Listen real good,
to the song of the blue bird,
to the drip of a faucet,
to the cricket playing its fiddle,
listen real good,
can you hear it,
A baby crying,
the bell of the ice cream truck,
childerns laughter,
now listen
as it fades away,
listen, as you can't hear,
the beautiful sounds around
fading to a whisper,
to be heard no more,
that is ,
the sorrow of a boy
losing his hearing
silence, never to hear
the music of his familes voice
silence, silence, silence

Tiny Daffodil

See the tiny daffodil,
dancing on the mighty hill,
little, but ready to fight.....
guarding the hill thru the starry night,
swaying in the morning breeze,
bright and yellow just to please,
See the tiny daffodil

The Plea

One day I got home,
all of a sudden you was gone,
Just a note to say good-bye
next to it your wedding ring,

As I sat trying to think,
what have I done to make you leave,
I gave you everything you could need,
Diamonds, Royce , house on the hill,

I never did a thing wrong,
went to work and came right home

So baby,
Plese tell me, so I know
what I done to make you go,

sitting here with my heart hanging out,
trying to figure it all out,

As I look out the window
a teardrop falls
I see two birds singing together,

All at once it dawned on me,
you left cause of me,
not for the things I have did,
but all the rest said undone,

When was the last time I said...
That I love you,
how much I need you,
Baby how I care for you,
Or gave a kiss just cause,
a hug to show my love

Baby if you where here,
I 'd show you how much I care
So Baby if you hear my plea,
OOOH baby come back to me

With a touch of a switch

With a touch of a switch,
the internet comes to life,
world is at your finger tips,
you sit and stare,
looking at the names,
wondering if they are doing the same,
wondering if just a touch,
you can be zapped,
to another country
to another place
to another time
is it better.... is it worse
sitting here wondering
sitting here thinking
with a touch of a swtich
the internet goes DEAD,
so does your connection to the world

Call

A phone call did ring,
News with it did bring,
news she thought....
could turn my feelings around,
news she thought.....
would make me slam the phone down,
News of other childern she did bear,
news of their adoptions her mother did take care,
two girls and a boy
all older then me,

since the phone call that Saturday,
a day doesn't go by
that I don't think of the others
two sisters and a brother,
do I let them all in,
Or keep them at bay,
that is the thought....
that runs through my mind every day.

What are they like,
how will they be
are they freindly
are they wicked , cruel or mean.

White Knight

Once up a time,
in a land not so far away,
there was a white knight
looking for his princss bright,
with hair of brown and eyes of green
with the sweetest smile he ever seen,
skin so fresh, lips like roses,
and her name so mystically it poses,
his love so deep, would sweep her off her feet,
it's time for him to open up,
by her maigical touch
the flowers will bloom, the skies will shine
the heavens will open, wit the touch of her hand,
now for her to tell him, make him understand
that the love she gives is pure as gold
so white knight open it up
let her see your love flow

How you feel

My heart is full it aches,
to tell you how I feel,
It was hurt once upon a time,
It's filled with so much emotion,
from laughter to being scared,
it throbs with wondering
how you feel for me,
baby when I'm with you,
it's like I'm in another world,
of wonder and rainbow,
of waterfalls and sunshine,
you don't know....
that you have the key to my heart,
tell me how you feel
to stop the ache of my heart,
let it over flow with joy
so tell my heart how you feel,
and open it up to the wonder
in it

My love

Love is in my heart and soul
it's love that will grow and grow,
only for my love that is true,
my body and my mind
will not do another
for it's made from birth to be just with you
it has had others,
but none that tunes it in like you,
god put you on earth to touch me deep,
put me there to mend the wounds
he saw the one I put on you
and gave me a chance to fix it to
he says my words are just not that,
the things they say are for a fact,
held for truth under his eyes
as he sees it for now and always
so baby here it is to tell you once more
and before the lord, I swear this so,
that you are the one and only
until we both grow real real old,
then I will hold you tight as I
move into eternity with you,
this is how I feel
my love is true
and it's held just for you

Stardust

Do you wish you could touch stardust,
what is it,
stardust , a speck of the galaxy,
stardust, a speck of heaven,
star dust, or is it a speck of a tired
star, falling to earth,
crying it's self apart,
as it falls from its home
stardust, a speck of mystery,
stardust, a speck of wonder,
is it there or.....
is there magic,
can you catch it
can I touch it,
is it cold.... is it hot..
soft, hard, smooth, rough,
star dust, as it falls it disappears,
for us to wonder about it,
stardust

All around

when I look around,
I do not see you,
baby you left one hot summer nite,
Loneliness engulfs me
and it is so strong
feeling the hurt of
no arms around me
you might not be here in person,
but ooh do I feel you
you're on the dust in the sunbeam
you're in the raindrops
falling on my skin,
and baby I feel you in the cool
summer breeze
when it moves over me,
as I see you in the dark starry night,
the twinkling stars,
the man in the moon
so no matter baby where you are
or who your with,
I will feel you always with me,
as I stand alone

Illusion

As see you standing there,
I wonder if it's an illusion,
I want to touch you to make sure,
But is afraid you'll disappear,
seeing you in the moonlight,
with the rays around you
watching, seeking for a sign,
your hand glides way out wide,
as my hand goes to touch
it goes right thru you
my eyes open wide
a tear comes to you,
you blow me a kiss,
and fades away
and there goes my illuions

Me

What is me,
a indivial with feelings,
like everyone else,
I cry, I laugh, and smile
but me, I'm also so alone,
even with a bunch of people around,
Me I'm shy, caring,
I share, In other peoples woes,
I'm a rock to hold on to,
A shoulder to cry on,
but me, when I'm down,
I hide it all, so no one knows,
The turmoil of my life,
I act so brave, even as I'm so
scared, of the unexspected,
what's around the next corner of
my life, should I reach out,
or hide with in,
I;m complex but so simple,
this is the real me

Mid-nite dream

Standing in a wide open field,
in a mid-nite summer breeze,
raises my face to the sky,
spreading my arms way out wide,
feeling the magic of the moon,
circling me in its cocoon,
white satin lace swayin,
to the music of the place,
as I start to spin,
slowly at first,
then faster, and faster,
my feet lift off the ground,
the wind takes me in
it's arms,
lifting me up and up
feeling like a butterfly
gliding on a stream of a
Mid-Nite dream
but so slowly it all stops
brings me down to the ground
opens my eyes
and lower my face,
thinking how wonderful it is,
to have the butterflies grace....
in the mid-nite dream

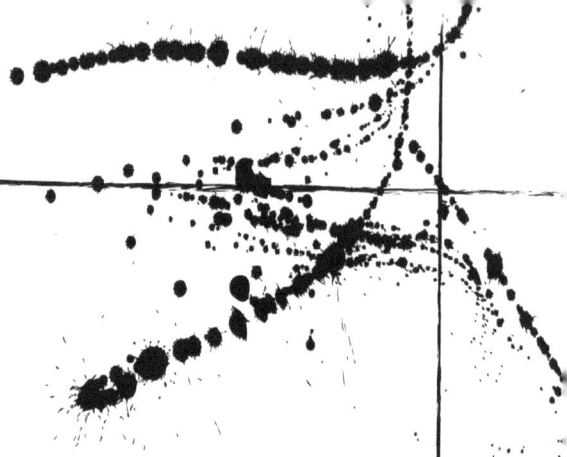

once upon a broken heart

Once upon a broken heart,
full of pain and sorrow,
sittin there all alone,
when then came upon the wings....
of the spring time breeze,
full of joy and happiness,
a mystic, magical essence,
a wonder... no eyes could hold,
swaying and twirling,
in a rainbow of sparkles,
it lifts up, and it comes down
stealing the pain and sorrow,
with a flash of brillance,
and a rain fall of sparks
it's gone once again,
on the wings of the...
spring time breeze,
onec upon a happy heart.

I love writing poetry, and reading.
My favorite authors are
Stephen King, Laurell K Hamilton

I Have two Handsome sons.. God bless
them.

Stephanie Harden

by stephanie A. Harden

Poetry to Ponder

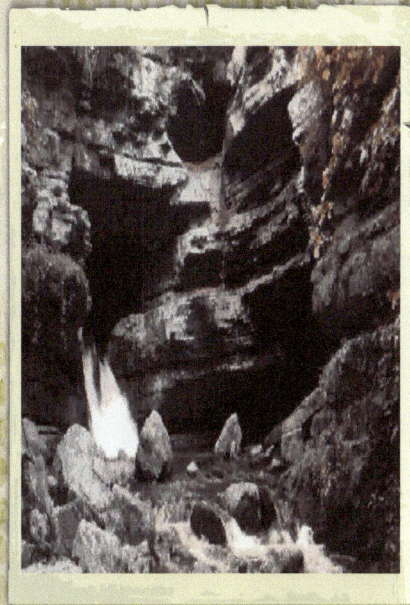

lulu

www.ingramcontent.com/pod-product-compliance
Lightning Source LLC
LaVergne TN
LVHW072107070426
835509LV00002B/54